CONFESSIONS
OF A
LONELY MYSTIC

SMALL TALK

CONFESSIONS
OF A
LONELY MYSTIC

SMALL TALK

Poems

By

MISHA HA BAKA

Confessions of a Lonely Mystic small talk

ISBN-10: 0-9987941-0-4
ISBN-13: 978-0-9987941-0-5

Published by Ha Baka Book

First paperback edition 2017

Dedication

For all that have
Taught me
Loved me
Helped me
Guided me
Protected and consoled me
Here now, before and to be
I give thanks.

Prologue

*Excerpt from a recently discovered
Ancient mystic manuscript*

What weakness lies within these walls?
Round heaven's child, a prisoner's stall.
To throw off these chains and be at rest,
To be one with Thee and all the rest.
Neither food nor drink does cheer the day.
But build these walls, which crumble as clay.
Upon my back, with eyes to the sun,
I await Thy will, not mine be done!
Night has come and crickets sing,
But my love for Thee is all I bring, for
Naked I am and naked will I be,
Till Thine outstretched arm encompasses me.
Till Thy will be mine, till with Thee I be.

Poems

small talk

2000 was a monumental year for the world. As it ushered all of us
into the next millennium, within me awoke a yearning to
reconnect to an inner self that had lain dormant for a while. I
searched for a medium to express the manifold thoughts and
feelings that were rummaging around inside of me. In the past, I
resorted to painting or music to do so. I had experimented with
poetry early on in life and occasionally thereafter. For some
reason, in February of 2000, my hand went to the pen rather than
to brush or instrument. I began writing many of the poems you
find in this collection of poetry. These poems reflect portions of
my inner me with minimum literary devices, hence I chose a part
of the title to be *confessions*. I have spent much of my life alone,
thus the addition of *lonely*. And last, but not least, I consider
myself to be a *mystic*. Much of my life has been spent in search of
God and the mysteries that come with that quest, therefore the
combination of *Confessions of a Lonely Mystic*. I have penned
several longer works, so I thought it best to subtitle this one: small
talk. I hope you enjoy delving into parts of my inner me and I
thank you for even being willing to do so.

Misha Ha Baka

A Poet's Dilemma

So you ask why I write now.
It's simple, easy to tell.
It's because I'm hungry.
Yes, that's it.
That will answer it well.

No, now that I think of it,
I've just eaten my fill.
I think it's because I'm lonely.
Yes, that's it!
That fits the bill.

What's that?
You are still unanswered?
I've already given my reply.
On second thought,
It was nothing but a lie.

Well, you see,
I've had free moments,
And thought I'd use them well,
But it seems you'll go unanswered.
There's really nothing to tell.

Cookie

A cookie
Makes you feel young.
Have you ever seen
An old cookie?
I have mine
With decaf.
It balances the youth,
But reveals the age.

A heavy sigh issues forth from my depths.
It lets out a cry of inner anguish.
As if abandoned in a barren wasteland,
Without signs.
I know I am love,
But can love be love without someone to love?
"Not this life," they said.
"You wouldn't want to do anything."
How ironic,
Since I don't know what to do anyway.
Music again?
Painting once more?
So I write.
Ask me, "Why?"
"Don't know" is all I can say.
Perhaps it is my legacy.
My small,
And I mean
Very small, token of thanks
For being here.
Trust me, it hurts.
Does it really matter?
Such a small token of selflessness?

A Wish

A simple thing:
A wake-less night.
From out of the blue,
I felt its might.
A subtle light,
Yet out of sight,
Wish I may,
Wish I might,
I couldn't fall
Asleep last night.

Body Parts

All body parts,
How fortunate we are.
Blessed be Thee, dear God.
That's not a battle
We need to make.
Blessed be the few
Who wander their ways,
With less than the rest,
Yet with as much at stake.

Amalgamated Conglomerate

Amalgamated conglomerate
Homogenate composite
Hydrophobic elixir
Solidified
Hardened
Leveled
Smoothed
Delineated
Defined
Baked with air and time.
Nature's abortion
Confined
Constrained
But easily refined!
No resilience here.
One yawn,
One sigh,
One laugh,
Or one cry
And shattered crevices asunder
Broken askew
Disheveled, up-heaved.
Gone false symmetry of motion
Contrived diminishing return.
Elemental compost.
A marriage of water and dust.
Adorned with smallest pebble.
A symphonic sea of crust.

The Gamut

As certain as I was,
Is as unsure as I now am.
I know I am me.
Entrenched in toys.
Surrounded with high-tech wonders.
I've reached the gamut
Of my non-connectedness.

Affirmation

I trust in Thee, dear God.
I believe in Thee, dear God.
I have faith in Thee, dear God.
I choose the path to Thee, dear God.
Now, always, in all ways, and
Forever.
Amen.

It's a Start

Disjointed symbols
Flutter in the air.
Erratic wings dart to and fro.
Lunging first towards the magazine stand,
Then the crowd.
Black wings contort,
Twisting and wrenching
In-flight
Struggling to stay airborne
And still, negotiate
The approaching crowd.
Nature knows no traffic green.
Its green is organic, not synthetic.
"Excuse me" is a dirty word in the city.
A catch-all for invasion of personal space.
"Excuse me, but you are standing in my spot."
"Excuse me, but can I have some of your money."
Another decorated polite-ism of deceptive intent.
A blackbird at 7:45 a.m.
Ominous.
The cigarette-smoking street guy
Allowed me to overtake him,
So that I didn't smell his pollution.
Aggravated sensitivities
From a reformed smoker.
"Excuse me,
But I have a right to enter your body with my stench."
Then almost across

He catches up ahead
And bellows his addiction,
Right in front.
Such is the way to work.
A five-minute snapshot.
Click, click.
My hunger calls.
I'm off to a decedent cafe.
The good stuff has become bad for you.
The wrong stuff is now in.
I will treat myself this morning.
Gear up for the days orchestrated events.
The sun is shining,
It's a start!

Dust to dust.
Speck in the eye.
So inconsequential.
It's not necessarily what,
But where.
Equal.
Thought.
Drifts in
From somewhere in space.
We feel it land.
Examine it.

Double day,
Double night.
Double sleep,
Double bright.
Rested yawn,
How I yearn for
Sleep's delight.

Emotional Body

Emotional body
Endures the neglect.
Once let loose
It speaks its needs
In stream of talk
All tossed in heap.
Less sudden stop cease
Freedom found
To ease burden
Of silence bound.
Thanks
For opportunity
To ease comfort,
Future reader
Presence felt.

Everything Has a Home

Everything has a home.
Sometimes we forget.
They lay orphaned
Drifting unanchored
Tossed back and forth
Shuffling for moments of rest.
Submerged beneath layered deposits
Of bygone days and prior dumps.
Excavation and resurrection
Become the call words.
Aggravation and agitation the mode.
So easily cured.
To the left life
The other abandonment.
Not only for my desk
But also for my soul.

It Almost Felt Like Love

For a moment
It almost felt like love.
How coy is illusion.
How creative is deceit.
How subtle is guile.
Omission is no substitute for truth.
Yet all are entitled to their happiness.
This time I was smarter.
This time I saw it quicker.
This time I didn't have to wait,
　For it to come off in my hands,
　Without being told it was there.
Ah, beauty blinds to imperfection.
It is difficult to outwit outrageous fate.
Nature wins every hand.
All roads lead to cosmic plans.
I kissed her goodbye.
I could feel her regret.
Not my problem.
Not my issue.
Not my love.

Better or Worse

For better
  Or worse.
Not only wed
  To one's mate.
There is family
  And family
That need
  When it's too late.
So in good conscience,
Under the guise of love,
We assist those
  Who are needy,
As do with us
  Those above.

Gratitude

Thank Thee, dear God,
　For my excellent job.
Thank Thee, dear God,
　For my excellent health.
Thank Thee, dear God,
　For my safe, secure home,
Thank Thee, dear God,
　For all the wondrous, and comforting objects
That support me and make me comfortable and happy.
Thank Thee, dear God,
　For my excellent future.
Thank Thee, dear God,
　For my freedom.
Thank Thee, dear God,
　For all the excellent opportunities
That you provide for me for
Growth, expansion, and increase
Of my understanding of Thy light and love.
And thank Thee, dear God,
　For allowing and enabling me
To love Thee with all my heart,
My soul and with all
That I do, be and am.

Agenda

God has no agenda,
Other than God's own.
To be all that God can be,
And experience God's All of All.

He told me to call them,
"The In/Out Chronicles."
"In," because they were relevant.
"Out," because they occur in dream state.
He had qualities about him
Not easily digested.
You know the type.
Some people are smooth as
Vanilla ice cream and apple pie.
He was more like burnt toast,
Raw at the edges.
So the first "advice,"
As my father calls it, was to understand.
Some take on some of the worst personality traits
In order to balance it with some of the best.
I told him he had better write it down,
Or he would forget.
He went for a pen;
I woke up very, very tired.
It must have been a very busy night.

How devious is malicious intent.
How inventive is directed discomfort.
Think about it.
Within us
Around us
They struggle
It lies and waits
For ripe opportunity.
As now,
The doors open,
And a maniac enters
Screaming, preaching.
Shoving it down one's throat.
At the very moment this was said,
Goes the light out dead in the hall,
The same morning the boiler fails,
And no hot water to comfort
Sleep-deprived weakness due to
Internal invasion, self-inflicted
By minuscule soldiers marching
To the drum of a lightless band.
Soothed by the roundness
Of a small white pill.

Dilemma Man

How do I position myself?
In relationship to not being
Where I would like to be,
And not knowing
What it would be like
To be whom I really am.
So perhaps
One of the reasons
I'm not "there" yet,
Is because I truly don't have a clue
What "there" would be like.
So for the moment, you can call me
"Dilemma Man."
Doesn't like what he has.
Doesn't know what he wants.
Knows what he wants and doesn't know how to get it.
Believes everything he needs he already has,
Or will easily get.
And at the same time,
Feels
He doesn't get what he needs.
He could also be called:
"The Almost Man."
In so many ways
Almost accomplished.
Medium well.
A Well.

A Medium.
Almost.

How in a Moment

How in a moment, so much can change.
In an instant, a whole history of events can transpire
   To be played out upon the stage of time.
We've only chatted once,
For less time than it takes
To down a drink,
And yet as she said: "Feels closer."
She must be aware
Of the power of her beauty
Upon the longing few,
   Who dare to explore this new realm?
   It is a foreign place.
She calls it, "A sense of comfortableness."
Already I'm her sweetheart,
Already I'm her, "Hon!"
I could see that,
From the very first moments
When we met.
The embrace,
The kiss,
The long, timeless moment
When inexplicable suction held our breath,
Melded in excited bliss.
I could feel her full, strong body
Pressed heartfelt against mine.
With an intensity and passion
That wouldn't let up, or let go.

I would have taken her as we stood.

Right there in the airport

Amidst the muddling commuters.

As if by magic,

We would have been oblivious

To all but us.

I can still feel the texture of her bra,

The smell

Of her perfume,

The smoothness of her skin.

 It was difficult to sleep last night.

All the moments with her became compressed,

And in sum presented themselves.

All the moments on the train,

In her arms.

No Longer Alone

The day separated us.
I did manage to linger upon the touch and scent
Of her full lace, floral, black bra.
There are some women,
Who enjoy the femininity of being a woman
In ways that fit my formula.
Thin black straps.
Fingertips exploring
Texture,
Contour,
Fullness.
Cupped palms in unison
Complete the dream.
No wonder the distance is great.
Otherwise, I might be undone.
I am no longer alone.
Well,
At least not for the moment.

How wondrous,
A sleep-filled night,
A humidity-free morning,
An empty subway car to work.
One hundred odors wafted.
Bright blue skies,
Fluffy white clouds,
Pristine clear air
And a pretty face to boot.
How glorious the world looks
Upon a rested wink,
A good day's weather
And a trouble-free morning.
Rejuvenated, revitalized, refreshed.
Able to endure
The programmed flow
Of incessant interruption
Insidious confrontation.
Cornucopian concoctions
Dance across
And ushered out.
How subtle is its work.
How easily beguiled.
Vigilance, fellow traveler.
Be wary
Of geeks bearing purloined
Emails touting unbridled

Wealth, fortune
And wanton sex.
From one to another
And back again.
Monotheism vs. plurality.
I didn't see it at first.
Then the truth I did behold.

I Almost Caught Her

I almost caught her.
Twice in a day.
Towering above the rest.
Erect, straight, and tall.
Flowing, blonde tresses.
Statuesque, refined, impeccably dressed.
Wafting long dress slit up the side.
With nature's breeze lending mystery to excitement.
Eyes hidden by hair.
Waiting in anticipation for
  Partial silhouette to turn to full view.
It happens.
Delicate features, chiseled lines, penetrating assured focused eye
Stating:
  "From first look, I stand first to look,
It only gets better than that."
Not arrogance or conceit.
The same as with
The pebble and the stone,
The mountain and the hill.
Bettered by better.
Better than the best.
We applaud the greatest,
We applaud the heights.
For me, I choose the pebble,
It stands greater than the rest.

A Sign

I am searching for the thread.
That synchronistic link-all
To bind me back to my path.
I struggle within,
Back and forth,
On and off.
There are signs that show you,
That you are on your way.
This is a long stretch of Incognito Highway.
I try coming to terms with what happened,
How I moved away.
Drowning myself in my music.
Deafening my ears to all but me.
And now I presume
That all that I have thrown away will be regained?
More arrogance?
Wishful thinking?
I try remembering the vibration's feel.
The mental and emotional high.
My position is still unclear.
Was it because of the link with her?
To see my dreams made mainstream,
In plain public view?
Perhaps it was my purpose then,
To set the stage,
To let others play.
And yet a part of me,

Feels greatly betrayed.
Dear God I pray for a sign,
That Thou show me how,
To find my way
Back to Thee and the Divine.

I Am Weary of the Night

I am weary of the night.
Too many scares and dreams of screams.
Too many wrenches from deepest sleep.
Too many efforts to once again
Enter a realm craved by body whipped
Too often and too long.
Abuse wears a crooked smile.
Assistance is a setup in disguise.
How sweet the forbidden fruit
Lulls complacency into resignation
Of an outrageous fate.
The morning fog covers the pre-dawn mist,
Which shrouds the twilight dew.
I can cut through with resistant eyes.

I Wait for Hers

I feel it as a struggle.
I feel it as a pull.
A tug between the light of love,
And toss betwixt the body full.
It wants to eat,
It wants to be thin.
It cries for sleep,
I'm pulled from my dreams,
I wish to soar to heights,
Fear feeds my weaker thoughts.
I've tamed the cravings for companionship.
But how I moved from Mystic Path
To complacency, still escapes me.
So my dear God,
Regardless of what I've asked for in the past,
I now ask for what is best.
I truly question what passion is left.
Toys still tickle my fancy,
But not too full.
I need a love.
I need a life.
So you see what perplexes me,
No sooner state conquered,
It returns in force as a need.
I know my life or what it has become.
I wait for hers.
I hope it comes soon.

The Big Pomegranate

I forgive them.
It is hard to be strong.
All, but a moment of weakness.
How subtle the influence.
They are signs.
I've returned to my path.
It can occur in an instance.
Vigilance is the word.
From an unexpected quarter.
From sincerest friend.
The elephant moves
Both forward and backward.
A crack is non-discriminatory.
They know not what they do.
They hear it as a joke,
Or see it as a flash of anger,
A lapse of memory,
A small inconsequential loss.
Such is life in the Big Pomegranate.
He instigated, I got blamed.
God gives to those who can handle it.
Amen.

I Know It Is There

I know it is there.
Something of my own.
Something different.
Something new.
Something that will truly contribute
To make a better you.
So many times I thought I found
  The meaning planned.
To only discover something else is there.
I am in an in-between place.
In-between purpose.
How sweet the exhilaration of purpose found.
How exciting the rush of meaning explored.
How drab recuperation occupies
Tired limbs and weary souls.
You have aged when you look upon youth and say:
"If you only knew the preciousness of your age."
But then again,
If we knew then what we now know,
Would we still be who we are?
Sometimes I start to think of who I could have been.
It lasts for but a moment.
The me that I am does not want to change.
The spirit is willing to become another I.
And yet a strong part resists and says,
"The dice have been cast, just play the round."
I hate waiting for the Dealer to deal.

I Truly Most Have Strayed

I truly most have strayed too far.
A day has past and no word from above.
No wonder that connection once felt strong,
Diminished now returns in momentary drones.
Awakened from sleep.
All those lost moments,
All those years lost in defeat.
My salvation lies with hope,
Once gained, not forever fully lost.
Perhaps as if in battle,
One contest lost,
Renewed strength determined,
Conquest sought.
Perhaps rest needed,
And creative fruits to bloom,
Bring meaning to my detour
And lift my ominous gloom.
I hope there will be others
To assist me on my way,
I pray for forgiveness
I pray for the day,
That once again you allow me,
In your house to stay.

Late

I let loose the reins
  That bridle the day.
I stopped the alarm
  From cackling its croak.
With intent and decision
  I went late to work.
How deliciously wondrous
  Were those thirty minutes of sleep.
Without worry of ramification,
  Without concern.
After two years
  Of being on time,
It was time to let time
  Idle by
And let sleep
  End its way.
And wouldn't you know it,
As it should be,
When I get to the train,
It too is late, just like me.
It too decided
  To make hay with the day,
To let loose its fetters,
And have its own way.
So now when the Boss asks me,
Why were you late?
I can with good conscience answer,

For the train,
I did wait!

I used to be cool.
Leather jackets, pointy shoes.
Nifty hats and pressed pants.
And now,
  You ask...
Well, I really can't say who I've become.
I am someone who isn't me.
It is as if I lost the me that I was and knew,
  Way long before I became the me that I am.
The clothes no longer fit.
The redefinition of outward self daily defined.
The major relationships translated into tens of pounds.
The major events buffered with ounces of fat.
How good it feels going down.
How sad it feels suiting up.
So many turns turned wrong.
Like ancient melodies
With faint glimmers
Of potential lives gone astray.
How certain I once was,
That, who I was becoming,
Was who I was.
How adamant I was
That who I was was who I am.
Now,
Perhaps the person sitting next to me
Has a better idea of who I now am.

Frankly, I don't have a clue.
I've reinvented self so many times.
At fifty, I once again search for me.
I've been medium in all that I do.
Blew it with music,
Blew it with art,
Even blew it with being medium.
With such certainty, each me thought it was I.
With such conviction, each I explored the new me.
Yes! This is who I am.
Yes! That is who I was.
It is hard being me alone.
With you, I could be an us.
Already there is definition.
And there too,
I can't remember
How many us' there have been.
Of course on Valentine's Day
It's hard to be a me
Amidst a sea of we's.
So there you have it.
The State of I.
The loss of we.
I miss the us, the you, and the me.

I Wait for It to Come

I wait for it to come.
The spark that lights the page.
The light that spins its web.
The particled threads unravel.
Chaos to mystical perfection in form.
I wait for a clue to follow.
For a word, or thought, or deed
That triggers heaven's message
For all below to read.
There are levels of visitations.
From in, to out, to midst.
I feel as though abandoned.
I feel as much betwixt.
I feel that I should tell you
All that I have learned.
But if you ask, to tell you,
There isn't much I've known.
No cures have I discovered.
No wonders have I performed.
I've walked into the Clouds of Heaven.
I've ascended the Mythic Stairs,
I've strolled with Guides and Teachers,
With the past and future, too.
Time is but a concept to move in, and out, and through.
I've lain with Spirit Mysteries,
And loved what isn't here,
I've flown beyond our planet,

Without a glimmer of a care.
I've seen the next dimension,
And heard its present toll,
I've walked amongst the angels,
And been spoken to by Soul.
Oh Spirit deep within me,
There is life left in these limbs.
Oh Creator in and out of me,
There is want still in my needs.
I ask that you inspire me,
To be the best that I can be.
I ask that you guide me,
To reveal the me within the me.
I ask that you assist me,
For without you I am naught,
But flesh and bones quite empty,
A house but not a home.
I ask that you make whole
What has drifted far apart.
I ask my life to be my life,
Being lived with all my heart.
I ask you not to desert me,
But let your love my channel fill,
Let me be your body,
Your mind,
Your heart,
Your will.
Oh, Inspiration I do call thee,

Fill me with God's love and God's light,
With God's wisdom, truth, and beauty.
Let me tell God's tales of wonder
And paint God's images of awe.
Let me heal God's tired children,
And reveal God's imaged plans.
Let me be all that I am destined,
As God's body and God's hand.
For without God I'm a pebble,
Buried deep within the sand.

Cold Turkey

I went cold turkey last night.
I was weaned off of my technological dependencies.
They were becoming idolized craven images
Not unlike that Golden Calf.
They are in perspective.
Beware the search for purpose
In a plastic circuit case.
Beware of Cyber gods.
Last night I returned to who I am.
I returned to who I was.
Today I am on the road
To once again becoming me.
I've done it before,
We can do it again.
Perhaps a clearing was
Necessary before being infused
With more of the real me.
I await the me that I am with open arms.
I thank the I that I am
For allowing me to once again
Move closer to being me.

Why Do It at All?

I'm at a loss,
As to what to write.
So it seems,
The words have left,
The desire is gone.
It is an effort
To search for call.
And I wonder,
Why do it at all?

If I Could Pocket a Smell

If I could pocket a smell,
What a world it would tell,
All the wondrous aromas,
Could work their way,
Into forgotten corners,
Forever to stay.

As a warm blanket
On a frigid night.

Inspiration

Inspiration has its own will.
Come as it goes,
Wants as it wishes,
Responds when it wants.
I search for the hidden road.
The unmarked path,
The thread that binds dissimilar events.
So familiar is this taste,
　Although clad in different attire over the years.
Of recent times, the dress of the populace.
In current, untrimmed, un-un.
No pride in my work.
No pride in my presentation.
Deserted by my aura.
My future seems but a dream.
The only glimmer that brings light to my heart,
　The prospect of a new toy,
　Or hearing from my distant sweet.
"Get a life," the poet ranted.
"Where do I start?" I replied.

The Body or the Wish

It always amuses me,
When I see,
A ballet dancer walk by.
You can tell.
There is the poise,
The balance,
The statuesque posture.
What brings a smile to my lips
Is the question of which came first?
The ballet body,
Or the wish to ballet?

It always stands out from the rest.
A clean spot at the edge of a rug and the rest is undone.
There she sits unknowing she is being chiseled in pen and ink.
Unknowing one hundred years from now
You will read of her journey home on a subway car.
On a dingy, humid, languorous February night.
Sitting, reading her book, she has become a star.
Not a brilliant one with followings,
And private life all lost,
But one of the constant ones,
Whose remembrance
Will long be present in quiet ways.
For you, she is as real as this day.
As the night, she was carved upon this page.
I look up and see she still is there.
Only seconds now until the last stop.
And all are off.
Yet her journey will long travel
Upon this page.
She is almost eclipsed by others at her side,
But it is her.
She is the one.
We have arrived.
The stop is here,
And now she's gone.

Last Licks

It is at the moments
When the guard is down.
Like right before sleep,
Or before going home from work.
Last ditch attempts
To raise the fury
And unsettle the peace.

Mistaikes

It is like a throttle on a car.
Increasing the vibrations speed.
I wonder if I am numb.
I don't feel the love.
I have made so many mistakes in this life.
I hope I don't blow away the years I still have left.

Perhaps It Is Real?

It's on again.
My distant love is there once more.
Only a few sentences spoken.
Only a few feelings spent.
She can feel it just as strong as me.
Perhaps it is real?
I hope it's not another Cosmic Joke.
I hope it's not a waking connection for sleeping B.S.
I hope it's not one of the:
"I know it's over before it has begun."
Or,
"I wish it were over, but I'll go for dinner anyway."
I can so feel her solidarity.
As if I've felt it before.
I can so feel her depth, her insight,
Her passion, her strength.
And she found me.
I await her pebbles on my window.
Breathless will be my response.

Ka Plunk!

It stays and waits.
Patience is its name.
It cares not if you pass it by unfettered.
It cares not if you pass it by unnoticed.
It cares not if you pass it by.
It stays and waits.
Waits for the moment.
Waits for the melted snow to freeze.
Its powdered face into a mirrored pool
Of lulled complacency.
And then it comes.
The wind in cahoots with the snow,
The sun in unison joins the moment.
Distracted by the glare,
Swayed by breeze you swerve.
And then you are caught.
Ah ha!
In an instant a purpose fulfilled.
You hear it first and then you feel.
A pull,
A coolness.
The mind quickly gathers the disjointed threads
And an image appears.
You wonder, "How bad?"
Anger starts to rise.
The heat travels fast.
A welcome friend to the cold.

You look down.
Ah ha!
A miss.
You've won!
In a moment of jubilant joy,
  In an instance of unbridled mirth
  And victorious abandonment,
  You let slip the tenuous
  Tethers that bind yourself …
Ka Plunk!
You are undone.
The snow, the ice, the slush
Bear witness upon your un-torn parts
That you've lost this bout
With insidious vicissitudes
Of random act.
And you wonder if the universe
Can be undone because you have fallen.
Caught by that which stays and waits.

Hors D'oeuvre

It was only a sliver.
It was only a glance.
A momentary glimpse.
A combination of color and mesh.
It was the wrong tint.
Too much brown.
Not enough black.
The texture was passable.
Not perfect, not the worst.
The portion was appetizing.
Just an hors d'oeuvre.
And yet, it was sufficient to minutely
  Arouse a glimmer of longing
Within sleeping limbs.
As quickly as it appeared it was gone.
Like a ray of sunlight
Shooting from darkened clouds
Darting back
Once again hidden from sight.
  And with the good fortune
To be smitten twice
Within five moments,
To my left appeared another racing part
More suited to my tastes.
  And then it was gone.

Thanks

My God is a good God.
A forgiving God.
A God of love.
I had strayed from God's arms.
And with one request to return,
God welcomed me back.
I thank Thee, dear God.
Now, always, in all ways and forever.
I thank Thee, dear God.
From the bottom of my heart,
From the depths of my soul,
With my entire mind, spirit, and will.
With all that I do, be, and am.
I love Thee, dear God.
I trust in Thee, dear God.
I believe in Thee, dear God.
And I have faith in Thee, dear God.
I thank Thee, thank Thee, and thank Thee, dear God.
Amen.

Next time I'll be smarter.

Next time I'll provide,

For great moments of comfort.

For greater rewards.

First Scene, Second Act.

Waiting for the curtains to open.

It's one of those plays

Where the actors don't know each other.

They've rehearsed their parts alone.

They know them to a T.

This T is waiting for a new part.

He feels it coming.

The props and scenery are being glided into place.

The lighting is changing.

The director is hiding in the wings.

Previously he's been more prominent in the production.

I suppose he feels more confident with me.

I'm the same.

Perhaps some of the others haven't arrived yet?

Perhaps we are waiting for the props to arrive?

I feel as though I've recently gone through

A purge of some sort.

Perhaps making room for the new?

Perhaps healing of the old?

Being the seasoned actor that I am,

Having played so many different roles,

I wonder what part is cast for me now?

I do however feel it coming.

Perhaps it is a job change?

Perhaps a new love?

Perhaps a new apartment?

Or maybe,

The change is within me?

I'll be transported to new heights.

Perhaps I'll meet a new teacher?

Perhaps I'll start to write?

I've had so many beginnings.

I've had so many starts.

So many up and downs.

So many in and outs.

So many parts.

It's time for the limelight.

It's time for love.

It's time for me.

To be known for me.

Next time I'll be smarter.

Next time I'll provide,

For great moments of comfort.

For greater moments of reward.

The Blonde

No taller than perhaps 4'10",
But with a vengeance.
The tall, pretty blonde from down the station,
Walks a whole car length to stand next to me.
We enter the overcrowded car.
I think to myself, perhaps this will be the day!
Then without a moment's hesitation,
The malicious one squeezes herself,
Between the Blonde and me.
Into a space that shouldn't have been.
Into a non-existent space.
She begins the tormentous ride for the Blonde.
Turning, jabbing and pushing into her.
Taking whatever anger
Or multifarious influence is upon her
Out—onto the Blonde.
The Blonde looks momentarily at me.
I can smell the freshly brewed coffee
She holds in her hand,
And now wears on her coat
Thanks
To the little one.
The ride is strained,
All four minutes seem eternal.
I avoid eye contact with the Blonde.
The little one jabs me once.
I eye her,
But it wasn't directed at me,

Just a sideswipe at the Blonde.
Verbal shouts are exchanged.
The train stops.
The doors open.
The malicious one walks off.
Then with a deliberate pause,
She turns and heaves her bent elbow
Right into the de-training Blonde
Who startled, staggers off in the opposite direction.
This is at 7:45 a.m. on Monday morning.
The start of the week.

Enough

Not an ounce more,
Not even a smidgen.
Burned out.
Empty.
Overloaded.
Fried.
Stretched.
It's Friday night.
I'm ready to sleep.

Renovations

Once again I return to pen.
Or should I say stylus,
The times have changed.
So it appears it has subsided.
Perhaps there is no pressing need.
Or is there?
I can no longer take the speed?
I thought the lull was renovation caused.
Another few weeks and
That too shall be complete.
I fear I've strayed far from my path.
Knee-deep in the midst of life
With no apparent plan.
With only memories of foretold tales.
Promises of greatness seem more than I can do.
I suppose there are those who wouldn't want to invest
In one who refused to be the best,
Who chose to hide amongst the many,
And decline the glory of the few.
Or perhaps it is a momentary pause.
While renovations proceed within me, too.

Sleep

Only sleep draws me near.
I long to long for extra moments stolen from sleep.
The kind you used to steal from your mother before dinner.
So immersed in my work that I have no time for sleep.
Oh, the mistakes I've made.
Oh, the opportunities lost.
Forever gone.
This age comes no more.
This body will re-form,
But in another time and place.
This time is passed.
How foolish I've been.
I wish to seize the next golden opportunity.
Will it come?
When?
I wait.
I've been waiting my entire life.
Waiting for it.
Waiting for *her*.
I no longer trust who I am.
How could I have made such a shambles of my life?
So much there and nothing to show.
I am tired of living someone else's life.
I want a life of my own.

A Good Day

Overload occurs early in the day.
Hundreds of angry faces yearning to be elsewhere.
One can look down to avoid the barren stare.
One can ignore their invasion
Of personal space
And allow a strange arm to grace one's own.
Then the race for the seat.
The coveted prize of a morning quest.
It requires agility, grace, and skill.
Voila!
Success!
Of course, it is the aisle seat.
The hand rest to support the weary limbs.
On a good day, no one intrudes on one's space.
On a good day, the sunrise is at one's back.
On a good day, no chatterboxes
Break the solemn solitude
Of all those
Who are transported
To their appointed rounds.
The trip home tells the tale.
It was a good day.
Amen.

Rock, Paper, Scissors

Rock, paper, scissors, cut.
It is the stone that stands on top.
No need for dimension.
Sufficient just to mention
　Its nature and it wins.
Yet that which is thin,
Can cover its sides,
　All over its hidden
　Weight cannot be denied.
What's unseen can be felt.
Its presence bears witness
To an ancient past.
Primordial in nature,
Prolific in count.
I seek the ancient echoes,
　Turned solid, set in stone.
Those molecules of mystery,
　That nourishes skin and bone.
Swirling streams of essence,
Streaming curls cntwined.
Twisted perfect sequence,
Destined futures aligned.

Nap

Saturdays are meant for naps.
The sweet taste
Of soon to be found sleep.
The familiar yawn
Of recently awakened craving for repeat treats.
The body enjoys a yawn.
It swells up from deep inside.
Muscles expand, contract, and avoid forms.
In truth it is nothing.
Absence of form.
A huge cry for attention.

Silver Silver

Silver cup,
Silver spoon,
Silver sunset,
Silver moon.
Silver memory,
Silver prize,
Silver silver,
Silver sighs.
Silver evening,
Silver cries,
Silver moments,
Silver eyes.
Silver silver,
Silver whys?
Silver whispers,
Silver byes.
Silver dust,
Silver song,
Silver silver,
For you, I long.

So I come to the cafe to write.

Hoping to connect with someone.

It's empty.

One has her back to me.

Running child.

Discordant music.

Drafts blowing wild.

There is nothing like being

In the wrong place

At the right time.

So many couples.

So many friends.

So much laughter.

So many smiles.

Just you babe-stylus and me.

Loneliness seems to be my style.

I can just hear it now,

"But remember you will be alone a lot."

"You are exploring being you."

"No problem," I said.

It's been my way.

"It will not come 'til later."

"No problem," I said.

"I can wait,

It's been my way."

"You'll have to wait to meet her."

"But, there will be several before you do."

"I'm used to waiting."

"I'll enjoy the loneliness meanwhile."

In several moments the place has filled.

Now dozens of lonely faces,

Looking every which way.

Except straight at you.

Except for your way.

No eyes meet.

No gestures.

No contact.

No play.

Even though,

I am pleased.

I feel productive.

I've started my day,

By sharing my moments with you.

Thank you,

Dear reader,

For coming my way.

For allowing me to speak with you.

For sharing my morning.

For making me feel

There are eyes watching,

Noticing,

And hearing what I have to say.

But truly, if you asked me,

"Do you have anything new to share?"

I'd have to answer,

"Not really."
I've heard it said before.
Not much new here.
Very little I could contribute
In a novel way.
Everything changes.
Yesterday, I was certain.
Today, I no longer know.

Vacations

So it seems it has shifted again.
From moments of destitution,
To hope for the future.
Be careful of your thoughts.
Be wary of your beliefs.
Trust in your dreams,
Do not abandon them.
Trust in yourself.
All is not lost.
Pick up the pieces and start afresh.
The obvious is not always what is occurring.
Sometimes it is.
Tame the hunger and cleanse the mind.
Poetry is a short vacation
Into another place.
Travel often.
Forgive your mistakes.
How quickly they change.
Now present, now gone.
Who knows when next
I'll be inspired to write.

Whispers

The sounds of clicking heels,
Slurping nostrils,
Of birds, and planes, and passing cars.
Of a rolling stroller,
Voices drifting,
Idling engines,
Shuffling feet.
Ah, a bump.
An ancient motor toil,
Ah, a crow cries,
Wild geese fly by.
The wind,
It whispers in my ear.
I sigh.
How wondrous this world is!
Both seen and unseen.

Jazz

Sunday morning,
At the coffee shop,
Rain drizzling,
Mist falling,
Cappuccino echoes off the walls.
Jazz plays above,
Weekend papers gently rustle,
As I sit by the window,
Watching the world pass by.

Return

The only thoughts that occupy my mind
Are how precarious was my pursuit.
I think I was well guided,
But there is arrogance within me.
Ego wanted to shine.
Prematurely, I suspect.
All gained was all lost.
It has taken me five years
To recover from the blow.
And once again I begin anew.
I hope I haven't permanently deserted my destiny.
Last night gave signs of a possible return.

The focus has shifted,
The field of view has expanded.
As best as I can make out,
I was lost in the Elysian Fields.
The mental realms,
The lower portions.
There are levels.
The Astral planes.
It has a new name this time.
Multi-leveled,
Out of context,
Wish fulfillment,
Instant gratification,
Source of untold wealth,
Instrument of knowledgification.
Five years lost there.
Perhaps,
I should look at it as a detour.
A chance to be myself.
An opportunity to be me again
After years of feeling them.
I was too free.
I was too innocent.
I was too open.
I was too arrogant.
I was too soon.
And still, they mock me
In a gentle way.

It's okay.
I welcome their play.
Fear still persists.
A Hydra of revelations.
How subtle the guise of
That Which Is Not.
How easily at times,
That Which Is falls folly to its prey.
Grant me the wisdom, dear God,
To be able to perceive, understand,
And differentiate between the two,
With ease, peace, and comfort.
And grant me the strength
To walk my path with Thee, dear God
In love and light.
Amen.

The road began to swirl.
At first slowly, then quickened.
It elevated and swerved from side to side,
Ever lifting upwards.
It did so for several moments
And then it lifted to the sky.
And a shaft of light
Like a pillar
Descended from the sky towards me,
Swirling.
And it did so for several moments.
It rooted itself upon me.
Surging light within.
Entering from the solar plexus.
I vibrated strongly for moments.
I was used to the process.
It stopped.
And then,
I opened my eyes.

The slightest glimmer,
  The slightest glance,
  Brings thrust to saber,
  Brings ink to stance.
En garde!
I hear its call.
Can my muse be summoned so early?
At just past dawn?
A feeling, a thought, a touch, a sigh,
  All are available to make its
  Stay.
How strange it must be
  Given all that I've lived,
  Not to be able to tell
  All that there is.
Allow them their fantasy,
  Allow them their gloat,
  Allow them their failures,
  Allow them their defeat.
Perhaps several lifetimes,
  Perhaps at the end of time,
  Perhaps in the next moment,
  Or never at all.
Will it be available?
  Will it be known?
  For me, it seems lost,
And I'm still all alone.

This Soul

There are clues in the air.
On the ground, everywhere.
Upon their faces,
Writings written on the walls,
Sounds spoken in the halls.
Flashing lights,
For no known reason,
Children talk,
Foretell the future.
It is the Season for Descent.
People waiting for discord,
Others making the best of little.
Plucked a crystal from its roost.
Deep, dark, shiny,
Black as smoke.
Threw it back to spend its time,
Weaving spells on lives, not mine.
I am waiting for my message.
I am waiting for my sign.
I've been waiting a very long time.
There are constraints,
Constructs defined,
Curves, and circles, and straight lines,
I feel the boundaries of my present life.
They are pushed to the limits,
Or the walls would smoke.
Compressed, restrained, familiar plots,

I seek new freedom to grow and learn.
Yet these muscles are tired,
They are resistant to yearn.
They no longer respond in familiar ways.
I feel my age.
I feel my failures.
I feel my feeling diminish,
Yet nothing returns.
The mind still wants.
The body still sways.
The heart is willing,
To change its ways.
Oh, Holy Mother.
To Thee, I pray,
You understand the need for,
Feminine,
For love,
For want,
For fun.
Oh bring to me meaning,
Purpose and relief.
This soul is tired of shuffling,
In anguish and deceit.

There Are Signs That Give the Day Away

There are signs that give the day away.
Waking at four a.m. dreaming of work,
  Then staying awake 'til six.
The hot water changing
Right when you are ready to indulge
In a moment of reverie with eyes closed.
  At the station she puts herself right in front of you; she isn't your
  type.
  She pokes you with her bag, and the train is empty.
  The regular sandwich guy is playing hooky.
  The regular checkout girl is playing sandwich guy.
  She thinks cream cheese is jelly
And gives you a rose instead of a snowball.
  The owner is playing checkout guy.
  He forgets to total the last sale
And charges $5.95 for your rose sandwich and white, black coffee.
  You tell him, "I think there is a problem."
  He doesn't understand English and smiles, saying, "$5.95 please."
  You point to your now undesirable breakfast and to the register.
  He frowns and takes five minutes to add the two items.
  It takes another five minutes to figure out how to cancel and
  retotal the sale.
  You are now late for work.
  You arrive to hear a message
Telling you that the dream girl
You offered your assistant job to
Has refused the position.
  It's not even nine a.m.

There are signs that give the day away.

There Are Smells That Stir the Soul

There are smells that stir the soul.
Odoriferous, triggered endorphins dance in joy.
A wood-burning fireplace on a cold morning.
Freshly brewed coffee and Sunday newsprint.
The approaching scent of a walking woman.
A fine cigar and martini, with a twist of lime.
Sliced peaches with strawberries and cream.
Raw cologne slapped on freshly shaved cheeks.
Minty toothpaste mouth and baby's breath.
Fresh cut grass and blooming rose.
Pumpkin patch, pumpkin pie,
Thunderclap, pre-storm skies.
Pinecone forest, ocean surf,
Fresh, baked bread, steak 'n turf.
Matchstick sulfur, whiskey, and rye,
Bagels and cream cheese,
Onion cries.
Incense, candle snuff, laundered shirts.
Horses, doggies, bubble bath,
Your mate's favorite scent.
And of all the smells intense,
Is that one whiff you take
After a cold has spent its course.
It is absence
That makes the snout
Grow fonder.

You Can Tell a Man by His Shoes

There is dignity in his face,
But poverty on his shoes.
Red rubber bands hold up tattered socks.
Shattered souls spread from battered facings.
His hat is worn as a royal crown.
Feathers proudly displayed echo a now gone era.
Scarf neatly tied as ascot,
Soiled canvas bag proudly worn on arm,
From head up, he could be mistaken for nobility.
From feet down,
Well,
As Mom always said,
  "You can tell a man by his shoes."

A Cobalt Sky

This morning I realized
How precious is each day.
How truly wondrous
In each and every way.
The clouds dance
Their orchestrated improvisations
Against a cobalt sky.
The cool fresh air
Runs its fingers across
All in reach.
Free to do as they please,
People
Scurry about
On their way to work.
I myself have a sense of relief.
My God has heard my prayers,
And allowed me
To return to God's house once more.
Last night I packed,
And began to move.
Two ferret-like birds
Were given to me as gifts.
At first, they were untamed
And scared.
They were molting
And though still sought
To roam on to themselves,

They became more comfortable
In my hands.
I still have to load up the vessels.
It is good to be alive.
It is good to study once more.
What wonders this world
Has yet to reveal.

Pets

Today a pigeon vied with the steam

To drag me from my dream.

Contrapuntal alternating slices of yanking tone versus hiss
dredging me from my wanted slumber.

How ingenious it is when It wants to get your goat.

Of course, It didn't stop there.

Once again my morning calisthenics consisted of shower bends
and grips wrestling with the heat of the steam.

Today was a good morning.

I only had to struggle with the shower's emotions and not its
physique.

A steady stream graced my back.

No tired trickle lingered on my wanting shoulders.

Flying rats.

And my radiator is a denizen of hissing snakes.

No wonder my building doesn't allow pets.

Today I foretold the future.

Albeit only three seconds in advance,

But still, I coined the phrase before it was uttered, so-to-speak.

I smelled the cigarette moments after I saw him light up.

I knew it was to occur.

I knew it would happen.

I was walking towards destiny.

I was walking into the future.

Today will be a leisurely pleasant day at work.

I've even brought my cameras to go romp around during lunch,
  taking pictures.

Both high guys are out, which leaves us next guys really on the
  top.

If only the rest of my life was as easy to read as those smoky few
  instances this morning.

I've elected to play it moment by moment,

Day by day.

What time will bring is a mystery.

No real plans made other than family events.

I have lived half a life thus far.

A partner of one.

A couple not yet fulfilled.

I patiently await my beloved.

I patiently await being the me

I would like me to be.

Today I foretold the future.

In a puff of smoke.

Late Start

Today was a late start.
Two hours lost in the night.
I hate when that pulls me from sleep.
Lately, I'm into sleep.
Not creating, but sleeping.
She keeps crossing my mind.
Is it her thinking of me,
Or me thinking of her?
An absentee relationship.
Is it better than none?

A Dream

Weekend mornings are tough.
So many choices, so many thoughts.
Today I opt for my favorite French cuisine.
At a little bistro off the avenue.
One of my favorite themes is playing.
My mind sifts through the day
Searching for a point to focus its purpose.
It keeps drifting back
To the short-haired, thin woman
On the bus last night.
It felt good to be held again,
Even if it was just a dream.

Another Realm

What if there was another realm.
Laid secret, hid in mystery,
Unknown, but to a few.
Not filled with Spirit Issue,
Or Space Being World.
What if there was a different
Concept truly true?
With consciousness of purpose,
The fuel of all the worlds.
What if this other Isness,
A Universal Mind,
Directs the very essence
Of all there is to find?
What if this substance,
Intelligence defined,
Exists with own purpose
Unlike another kind?
What if this concept,
Isness of All That Is,
Was what we call Divinity?
The Is that always is.
What if a certain someone,
Could enter into call,
Could enter in communion,
With this All be All to All?
Then he could summon the universe.
He could call the mountain tall.

He could turn the day to night,
And turn oceans into walls.
He could walk among the destitute,
And heal the sufferer's plight.
He could see the past and future
As easily as present sight.
He could come and go between us
From this realm to the End.
The Alpha and Omega,
Even light could he bend.
There are those who walk among us.
There are those who have walked before.
Who talk to Is of Isness,
Who walk within its doors.
For me there is dilemma,
Coupled with remorse and regret.
To have tasted Isness' Isness,
And have chosen to forget.
I wonder what magic,
What spell, potion or brew?
Drew me from my beloved.
How sad, how anguished, how true.
I walk among the many,
This time I will not sway,
Hoping to regain,
What once was there about me,
I almost walked away.

What Is An Actor Without a Part?

What is an actor without a part,
A hero without a war?
A barber needs hair,
A teacher, students,
An angel, someone in need.
Creativity, a canvas,
A musician, an instrument.
A programmer, a language.
The giver, the receiver.
The theory, the act.
So where does that leave me?
Somewhere in between?
So many mistakes.
Have I chosen a coward's path?
Have I lost my way?
Midway in life
I feel less certain
About my future
Then when I was eighteen.
I've spent so much of my life
Being there for others.
And yet, so much of my life
Being with myself.
Why, given all my history,
I've made the choices
I have,
Is a mystery to me, too.

Mountain

What school then
  Did Mountain attend?
Was it Hill first?
  From there to ascend?
Or did it start from dust,
  With eons drifting by,
To emerge a pebble,
  That's destined for the sky.
What patience rests within?
  To endure time's long test.
Or is waiting but a notion,
  To secure us at its best.
Perhaps it knows not changing,
  Or to it, it is a cell.
Like us when we were children,
  Who now have grown to tell,
That we stand high as mountains,
  In God, we place our trust.
That we were once as pebbles,
  Compressed by time from dust.

Rhapsody

When you go for a walk,
The universe is your home.
The trees are about to spring into Rhapsody.

Forever

Yesterday there was a future.
Today there is the past.
Yesterday there was romance.
Today it no longer lasts.
Yesterday she loved me.
I can feel it clearly today.
But today she's gone forever,
  Forever and away.

Imagine

Yesterday it was over,
 Today it has begun.
Renewed hope is flaming,
 Hopefully, it won't run.
Only a mere sentence:
 "How close do you want me to be?"
Imagine the answers.
Imagine all I'd want to see.

So I write her a missive.
A token of my want.
I wait for its answer.
The moments seem so long.
Rhythms echo in my mind,
Rhymes jingle and search for place,
I struggle to position my feelings
 Amidst a sea of discordant mist.

Clueless

You ask my plan,
My vision for my life?
What will be in five or ten,
Or perhaps today?
As if horse with blinders,
I don't have a clue.

Sunglasses

There are some things that just shouldn't be.
Perfection so early in the day.
Too bright for the eyes to behold.
Sunglasses ease the blow.

Black leather motorcycle jacket.
Long blonde platinum hair.
Skin tight, black leggings.
No skirt.
No pants.
Just a small, tight, exquisite, round rump.

I race in front of the handheld pair.
He claims her with his grip.
She states, "I'm taken" by hers.

They enter the brightly lit subway car.
Fluorescent lights blazing above.
I'm happy I was wearing
Sunglasses today.

Here,
Sitting with my
Mind in my hand.
I watched,
Craving to hold,
To press.
Starvation
Trickled down into
My empty stomach.
Seizing upon her slightest
Gesture.
It cried within me,
Go speak
Smile,
Signal.
I remained dead.
My mind spun
On
A solid immobile carcass
Remaining unmoved.
"Why?"
Clang in my ears,
And ripped my insides.
A few steps away,
Oh the pleasure to hold
To press, to caress.
"Why?"
Raced in my blood,

And made my head swoon,
"Why?"
Knotted my stomach,
And buzzed in my ears,
My pulse raced,
My guts grumbled,
My head ached with noise,
Hurt by that illusionary anguish
That separated us.
She looked so old.
I could feel it.
She would just laugh, or smile,
Or maybe even form
A platonic hold.

Tomorrow

My thoughts flee
From empty tombs,
Crowded book, and
Soft-dead-spoken preacher, teachers,
Restless-quiet,
Summer swept streams.
Slashing through vegetated blackboards.
Carrying a dream, drowned, diver away.
Beneath, below, and out.
Where?
He steals upon a drip-flow
Off.
Weathered, warm, colored, clean
Tingling cries of
Bicycles charging through school rooms rotted
Bouncing giggles, excite steams—stoned.
Carves air with wild, wet, wide lips.
Alive tomorrow.
Four days to come.
To taste definite leaves of white, cloudless, blushed trees
Upon her face.

Interstellar Light

Interstellar light shines forth.
Life long-lived
Lives again
Eternal, dynamic.
Which is the real?
They see, but it was
If what once was,
But one can ask
When we see our friend,
"Is it not light
That strikes our eyes?"
Therefore because time
Travels not between planets
We call it real?
Then we must say,
"The starry light must be real?"

Tiberius

I have left the house
To search for my home.

As I left my home
Then only did I see what it was.

They were all very sad.
So sad, tears were their blood.

And their tears filled me with anguish.
"Why?" To the heavens, I cried.

Then, only did I feel their love.
Their presence held in my tears.

Such sweet, sad tears.
My heart heavy, my throat full.

I lie upon the grass
The sky, my shield.

The wind, the caresser
The air, my life.

I have left my house
And now, I'm alone.

Desert

Listen!
"Can you hear the wind?"
"Can you touch its stillness?"

I see a man searching in the desert.
There is no one living to be seen.
His head is bent toward heaven.
But his lips are parched from the sun.

I see the wind
Come wiping down upon him.
I ask him,
"Any sight yet of town?"

He moans a scripture saying, "____,"
But the chasm has taken his words.

On his knees, I see him standing.
His life rent as is his shirt.

But to drink is written upon him.
Listen,
"Can you hear the wind?"

Masada

Much have I journeyed,
To stand at your feet.
Much have I struggled,
To prepare for your climb.
Bent back my head to heaven;
Still, see I not yet your design.

These thoughts dart before me
And already I have climbed,
As the sweat chills my body
And Spirit strengthens my spine.
In a moment still further,
But I look not behind.
Oh, how weightless is this body, and
How speechless is this mind.
When the future is the present, and
The present becomes the old,
When all three are together,
And together are a whole.
Then your summit will I visit
And your palace will I see
So far yet to journey,
Only time keeps you from me.

Silent stain drops
Dribble from my wet lips.
Sensuously sliding
Out of a yearning cavern.
Calling,
Crying,
They fall
To the dust.
Scattered
By examination of intellect.
Too mind,
Too scared,
Too withdrawn.
Upon carriages of compassion
They voyage a sea of economic scum,
Satiated only by some,
Some silent dew
Rising a sun
Will one day see.
Petaled stems bearing
Fruit to be eaten,
Or stored when
These tablets frown then
There are sensual symphonies
That caress with tender flakes of tissue
Silent stain drops.

The Choice

For when I want to go
Where I want where
Else can I go? I can
Only go one of two
Places, at first I can
Lead a life of free
Conscience and be
Free of everyone except
Myself or second
I can lead a life
Of wishes
Of the people with
Whom I play a role
In life! The
Choice is mine!
Or is it?

Destiny

With all that I have been,
How could it be?
That what I am now,
Is still,
But a fraction of me?
The me that I am,
Feels lost and astray.
The I that I am,
Feels confused and betrayed.
That which still seeks life within,
Prays for the chance,
  To once again begin.
It feels uncertain,
  This fate of mine.
I don't have a notion,
  How Destiny will unwind.
But know this for sure,
This vessel feels empty.
It feels despondent and grim.
It longs for the times
It was filled to the brim.
It longs for the moments,
That heaven did call,
To fill all its chambers,
Pathways and walls.
To have walked with the Ancients,
And now travel below.
Subterranean journeys,

Incognito woes.
Perhaps the sole purpose,
The main reason,
The main rhyme,
Is to provide you, the reader
With these poems of mine?
Or perhaps I have grievously failed,
Wasted a life,
And missed the call.
I hope, with all that still functions,
And with the strength still mine,
That I can contribute
And be worthwhile.
I've asked for a message.
I've asked for some signs.
I've asked for a teacher,
A new guide of mine.
To lead me to myself,
My destiny and the Divine.

What wordless worlds does beauty hold?

To lift the heart and noble soul,

Upon a gaze of calm serene,

To worlds but felt yet never seen.

Unwind sweet beauty and let me see

The worlds within most inner me.

But simple sights do me confound.

What hopes have I of depths profound?

Eternal struggle will I wage

Till sight of thee I do behold.

And if neither sight nor sense can I see

Descend with my soul.

What emptiness must within me lies.

If alone I am and alone I sigh?

Vapors rise and mists descend,

Like with like always trend,

But none with me time do spend.

Eternal Beauty
By The Lonely Mystic

Index of Titles

A

B

C

D

E

T

V

W

Y

PORTRAITS OF A LONELY MYSTIC
ILLUSTRATED NOVEL BOOK SERIES

THE LONELY MYSTIC
WITH HIS GUITAR AND NOSE RING COLLECTION

EXCERPTED FROM
PORTRAITS OF A LONELY MYSTIC IN 3D

THE LONELY MYSTIC

as Tiny Tyke...the saga begins

"I'M NOT IN A STROLLER, THIS IS A HIGH ROLLER!"

EXCERPTED FROM PORTRAITS OF A LONELY MYSTIC IN 3D

For my beloved, wherever she may be…

About the Author

Misha Ha Baka has worn many hats during his professional career. He has penned several other published works: Confessions of a Lonely Mystic short talk and a series of illustrated novels titled, Portraits of a Lonely Mystic. He has a BA in English Literature, an MA in Asian Studies and has studied healing and mystic thought in Asia, England, Israel and the United States. He is an ordained spiritual healer and an ordained member of the clergy. He is a fine artist, a graphic artist, a photographer, a musician, a composer and a music producer with dozens of albums of original music such as *Passion, Miracle* and *Ancient.*

www.ingramcontent.com/pod-product-compliance
Lightning Source LLC
LaVergne TN
LVHW091152080426
835509LV00006B/654